••• CLAIM YOUR FAITH AS YOUR OWN •••

OWN IT

28 DAYS TO OWN YOUR FAITH

➤ DISCUSSION GUIDE

AN IN-DEPTH, EASY-TO-USE GUIDE TO HELP YOUR SMALL GROUP
GO DEEPER ON YOUR FAITH JOURNEY TOGETHER

ON THE JOURNEY TOGETHER -

CADE THOMPSON &
SHELLEY FURTADO-LINTON

ISBN: 978-0-9908174-6-8
Printed in the United States of America.

Cover Design: Tim Murray, Layout Design: Shelley Furtado-Linton, Editor: Ann Lenaers
Although the author and publisher have made every effort to ensure that the information and advice in this book was correct and accurate at press time, the author and publisher do not assume and hereby disclaim any liability to any party for any loss, damage, or disruption caused from acting upon the information in this book or by errors or omissions, whether such errors or omissions result from negligence, accident, or any other cause.

CONTENTS

CONTENTS

ACKNOWLEDGEMENTS

To all the people that have poured into me over the years, I just have to say thank you. A few years ago, when I said yes to taking the calling of ministry upon my life, I really had no idea what that meant, now I am starting to understand what that means for me. I have to say thank you to my Mom and Dad for teaching me what it means to love like Jesus in a world that so desperately needs that truth. There have been so many leaders that have invested into me to be the man I am today, thank you for believing in me when some people thought I was crazy.

To any leader that feels like giving up on ministry, I pray that this Discussion Guide will reignite the fire within your soul to continue to share the gospel with people that are looking for hope. Never give up, you are making a difference.

INTRODUCTION

Hey, Cade here!

When the *Own it* devotional was first published, I was excited to see the response! So many of you have said it's helped you dig deeper into your spiritual journey.

I soon realized how great it would be to do the study as a group, but I knew a guide would make it easier to have group discussions.

That's when I reached out to my friend Shelley. She's written study guides for several books – including her own. Plus, I know she's as passionate as I am about helping others own their faith.

Together, we created this discussion guide that will help you walk alongside others as they uncover God's plan for their lives.

Life is so much better when we do it together. Now, you can use this study guide to help others go deeper in their relationship with the Lord.

Remember you are never too young or old to live out what God has for you, and it all starts with owning your faith!

Cade

GET TO KNOW THE DISCUSSION GUIDE

Weapons of Spiritual Warfare	**Overview:** begin each class with the weapons of spiritual warfare – prayer, God's word, and praise (worship music). This helps prepare the group for study time by: • Encouraging them to rely on God. • Helping them focus on the topic for that week. • Inspiring them to adopt these tools in their daily walk. **Prayer:** Bullets are provided as guidelines for weekly prayer; however, you are free to pray as needed. **Worship:** You may choose any song that relates with the weekly topic. In addition, a list of songs may be found in the playlist here:https://www.youtube.com/playlist?list=PLrdRKH vMsEz-tdP1nerpkMtoC6kGM8y1T **God's Word:** Scriptures provided relate to weekly topics.
Activities	A short activity is included that hints at the topic for that week. These activities are important because they help the group become comfortable opening up with each other in the group setting. Chapter questions are included as the last activity each week. Encourage volunteers to share their answers, questions, observations, or take-a-ways with the class.

Keeping It Up Week	The final week of the study is meant to help the group internalize what they have discovered and accomplished over 28 days. Several activities are included, but you can adjust the number used to the meeting timeframe.
Study Outline	**Week 1 – Setting the Stage** This week does the following: • Introduces the group leaders, the group members, and the study outline. • Prepares the group for expectations such as confidentiality. • Gives the group an introduction to the topics. **Week 2 – Getting Started** This week aligns with the first seven days of the study. **Week 3 – Going Deeper** This week aligns with days eight through fourteen of the study. **Week 4 – Making It Personal** This week aligns with days fifteen through twenty-one of the study. **Week 5 – Growing Your Faith** This week aligns with days twenty-two through twenty-eight of the study. **Week 6 – Making it Stick** This week makes time to celebrate and remember what the group has learned. It also prepares and encourages them to move forward in their faith. Make this fun!

WEEK ONE – SETTING THE STAGE

SET EXPECTATIONS

Say: We are here to:
- "Hear" from God.
- Learn and deepen our relationship with the Lord.
- Ready our hearts and minds so God can help us grow closer to Him.
- Be open to learn about:
  o Things we know.
  o Things we don't know.
  o Things we need to change.

Remind the group this is a safe space.

Say: We are free to share what is on our hearts. We may have questions, concerns, or doubts – and this is a safe place to be honest about those things.

Remind the group that privacy is very important!

Point out that in this group we are expected to protect each other.

Tell the group that any personal information shared should NOT be repeated outside the group, and remind them that gossip will not be allowed.

Ask the group for agreement.

Introduce the weapons of spiritual warfare.

Read this scripture out loud:

2 Corinthians 10:4-5
For the weapons of our warfare are not of the flesh but have divine power to destroy strongholds. We destroy arguments and every lofty opinion raised against the knowledge of God, and take every thought captive to obey Christ.

Say: Sometimes when we start to dig into our faith, it's like going to battle. We are going to wage "spiritual war" with the weapons of warfare, which are prayer, God's word, and praise.

Point out that every week the study will begin with the group preparing their minds and hearts with these tools.

Say: Let's use those weapons now.

Prayer
- God pursues us and wants a relationship with us.
- God is our defender and our helper.

God's Word
Ephesians 1:18
I pray that the eyes of your heart may be enlightened in order that you may know the hope to which he has called you, the riches of his glorious inheritance in his holy people.

Praise: <<Play a worship song of your choice.>>**ACTIVITY** 3 minutes

1. **Instruct** the group to take turns describing their best day ever.

2. **Ask** one or two volunteers to share how the experience they shared impacted their life.

Remind them they are going on a journey that will impact their lives in big, but good ways.

Encourage the group to commit to the process.

CORE CONTENT

Point out that every one of us is responsible to grow our own faith. We cannot rely on someone else's faith to get us by.

Say: Your mother, father, grandparents, friends, youth leaders, or others cannot own your faith for you.

Read this scripture out loud:

Ephesians 2:8
For by grace you have been saved through faith. And this is not your own doing; it is the gift of God.

Point out that by faith, we know God will help us grow in our Christian journey.

It's normal to have questions or fears about it. It's okay if we aren't sure how to grow our faith.

SAY: It's okay to wonder how this is all going to work. What is really important is understanding that even though we will each dig into our own faith; we will support each other through the process.

Explain that *Own It* is a devotional that helps us go deeper in our faith in a simple to understand way. It doesn't use fancy words or talk in abstract terms, and it doesn't require us to read Hebrew or Greek text.

This devotional is straightforward, and is meant to inspire you.

Point out there is one devotion per day. Each day includes a short prayer and a challenge.

Say: Starting tomorrow you will read one devotion each day for seven days.

Each week when we meet, we will discuss what you read and learned the week before.

Remind the group not to worry if they have questions, or if something doesn't make sense.
Tell them to bring their questions or concerns to the next group meeting, so the group can talk through them.

Encourage the group to complete each day's reading, prayer, and challenge. Remind them that God will be with them along the way.

Read this scripture out loud:

Deuteronomy 31:6
Be strong and courageous. Do not fear or be in dread of them, for it is the Lord your God who goes with you. He will not leave you or forsake you.

Point out that it is okay if this feels uncomfortable or strange.

Encourage them to dig into the study despite their feelings.

Say: Elephants are very large and strong animals, but they still journey in groups where they protect and support each other.

Point out that we are going to be like that for each other.

Explain that as a group, we will work through the questions in the devotional together.

Ask the group to go around the room and say one thing that scares them about this journey.

There is no right or wrong answer. The purpose here is to acknowledge any individual concerns.

Allow them to talk about what they feel. Acknowledge any fears that are expressed.

Encourage them to be brave and face those worries.

Read this scripture out loud:

Psalm 27:1
The Lord is my light and my salvation;
whom shall I fear?
The Lord is the stronghold of my life;
of whom shall I be afraid?

Ask the group to commit to surrounding each other in prayer and support.

WRAP UP

Remind the group that going forward they should read one devotion each day for the corresponding week.

Say: Over the course of the next week, you will read each daily devotion from Week One – Getting Started.

Tell them they will be answering the questions as a group next time the group meets.

Remind them that growing is a journey that never ends. Encourage them to commit to continuing the process with open minds.

Ask what questions they have.

End in prayer

WEEK TWO – GETTING STARTED

WEAPONS

Prayer
- The Lord is a light in the darkness.
- God doesn't just light where we are today, he lights where we're going.

God's Word
Romans 12:2
Do not be conformed to this world, but be transformed by the renewal of your mind, that by testing you may discern what is the will of God, what is good and acceptable and perfect.

Praise <<Play a worship song of your choice.>>

ACTIVITY
2.5 minutes

Introduce the activity by reminding the group that everyone is a work in progress, and everyone has good and not-so-good habits.

Say: Sometimes it's just as hard to start new habits as it is to quit bad ones.

Ask one or two volunteers to share a habit they would like to start.

There is no right or wrong answer here. Look for and acknowledge answers such as, eating better, exercising more, or other "good" habits.

Say: This study is a bit like developing a new habit. It takes time, and it means we have to stay focused.

Ask how the last week went for them.

Remind them it's okay if they didn't get to the devotional every day; however, they should continue to try to make it a habit.

Point out that doing something different takes time and commitment. We have to keep asking God to help us change.

CORE CONTENT

Read these scriptures out loud:

1 Peter 1:13
Therefore, preparing your minds for action, and being sober-minded, set your hope fully on the grace that will be brought to you at the revelation of Jesus Christ.

2 Corinthians 5:17
Therefore, if anyone is in Christ, he is a new creation. The old has passed away; behold, the new has come.

Point out how God promises that through Him, we *can* change.

Ask one or two volunteers to describe some things that make it difficult to change.

There is no right or wrong answer. The point is to get them to begin to self-identify reasons we sometimes don't do things differently.

Thank those who volunteered.

Ask the group to describe some things that can help them make new or better choices.

Allow one or two volunteers to answer.

There is no right or wrong answer; however, look for answers such as:
- Going to church
- Reading their Bibles,
- Spending time in prayer

Ask one or two volunteers to share the kinds of things that can *keep* us from changing.

There is no right or wrong answer; however, look for responses such as:
- We avoid reading our Bibles
- We watch, listen, or read the wrong things.
- We hang around with the wrong people.

Say: The only thing we can control is ourselves. We cannot change what happens *around* us, or *to* us, but we usually have the opportunity to make different choices.
Point out the good news is that God will continue to help us make better choices going forward.

Encourage them to continue to press into the process.

ACTIVITY

Answer questions as a group.

1   On day three, you learned how God feels about you. You were challenged to find a verse that talked about how God feels about you.

Share that verse with the group.

2   On day five, you learned about faith. The challenge asked you where it is difficult to trust God.
- What is one way it's difficult to trust?
- How does faith help when we struggle with trusting God?

3   On day six, you learned about grace. You were challenged to write down some ways that God has shown grace in your life.

Share one way He has shown you grace.

4   On day seven you learned about mercy. You were challenged to write down three examples of how God has shown you mercy.

Share one example of how God has shown you mercy.

WRAP UP

Say: No matter what has happened in the past or is going on in your lives right now, there is always hope for an amazingly good future if we make a choice to walk by faith in God.

Remind the group that God loves them! He wants them to live with victory over sin and brokenness, and to possess His promises for their lives.

Read this scripture out loud:

Galatians 3:13
Christ redeemed us from the curse of the law by becoming a curse for us.

End in prayer

WEEK THREE - GOING DEEPER

WEAPONS

Prayer
- God created us.
- God knows us inside and out.

God's Word

Daniel 2:22
He reveals deep and hidden things;
he knows what lies in darkness,
and light dwells with him.

Praise <<Play a worship song of your choice.>>

Ask how the last week went for them.

Acknowledge responses and encourage the group to keep going.

ACTIVITY
2.5 minutes

Ask volunteers to share one activity, hobby, or skill they would like to learn.

Acknowledge their answers.

Ask the group this question:

What do you think stops people from trying new things?

There is no right or wrong answer. The goal is to get them to start recognizing why they may be held back from going deeper with God.

CORE CONTENT

Point out that there are many reasons people avoid new things. Many times, fear is what keeps us from doing something we aren't familiar with and have never tried before.

Ask one or two volunteers to share something they are good at (music, dance, sports, art, etc.).

Acknowledge responses.

Ask the volunteers who answered to raise their hand if they are happy that they took the time to learn that skill.

Say: Most of us – if not all – feel uncomfortable or scared when we start something new. But, usually, if we push past that fear, we end up glad we kept going.

Read these scriptures out loud:

Luke 6:48
He is like a man building a house, who dug deep and laid the foundation on the rock. And when a flood arose, the stream broke against that house and could not shake it, because it had been well built.

2 Timothy 3:16
All Scripture is breathed out by God and profitable for teaching, for reproof, for correction, and for training in righteousness.

Ask the group to share reasons why they believe it's important to go deeper in their relationship with God.

There is no right or wrong answer. The goal is to get them to reflect on the importance of a deeper walk with the Lord.

Point out that everything that's alive must be fed in some way. Whether it's a plant or a pet – if they aren't fed, over time the outcome will not be good.

Say: As Christians, God's word is how we "feed" ourselves.

Read these scriptures out loud:

1 Peter 2:2
Like newborn infants, long for the pure spiritual milk, that by it you may grow up into salvation.

Point out that is why it's so important to have time with the Lord every day.

John 6:51
I am the living bread that came down from heaven. If anyone eats of this bread, he will live forever. And the bread that I will give for the life of the world is my flesh.

Jeremiah 3:15
And I will give you shepherds after my own heart, who will feed you with knowledge and understanding.

ACTIVITY

Answer questions as a group.

1 Day eight talked about the unreliability of our emotions.

   Why is it important to rely on what God's word says rather than our emotions?

2 Day nine and ten talked about the truth of God's promises and how they are true for you. You were challenged to find promises you can relate to.

   What is one promise that you know is true for you?

   Note: If the group hesitates, share your own verse.

3 Day thirteen talked about living a life of gratitude.

   What is one thing you are grateful for?

4 Day fourteen talked about the importance of thinking about the right kinds of things.

   What are two ways you can change your thoughts?

WRAP UP

Say: No matter what is going on around us, we can trust God's word.

Remind the group that God loves them! He wants them to live with victory over sin and struggles and to hold tight to his promises for their lives.

Say: The good news is God is patient and merciful. He will continue to help us as we learn to draw close to him.

Read this scripture out loud:

Philippians 4:6
Do not be anxious about anything, but in everything by prayer and supplication with thanksgiving let your requests be made known to God.

End in prayer

WEEK FOUR – MAKING IT PERSONAL

WEAPONS

Prayer
- God wants a personal relationship with us.
- God knows everything about us.

God's Word

John 5:24
Truly, truly, I say to you, whoever hears my word and believes him who sent me has eternal life. He does not come into judgment, but has passed from death to life.

Hebrews 4:12
For the word of God is living and active, sharper than any two-edged sword, piercing to the division of soul and of spirit, of joints and of marrow, and discerning the thoughts and intentions of the heart.

Praise <<Play a worship song of your choice.>>

Ask how the last week went for them.

Acknowledge responses and encourage the group to keep going. Continue to encourage individuals who still struggle with completing the daily devotion.

ACTIVITY
2.5 minutes

Ask volunteers to describe their best friend in three words.

Acknowledge their answers.

Ask the group to describe a stranger in three words.

Acknowledge responses.

There is no wrong answer here. The goal is to get them to understand it is difficult to describe someone they do not know well.

CORE CONTENT

Ask several volunteers to describe the difference between true friends and acquaintances.

Acknowledge responses.

There is no wrong answer here. The goal is only to get them to begin to see the difference.

Say: God does not want us to be acquaintances. He wants to have a personal relationship with us.

Read this scripture out loud:

John 15:5
I am the vine; you are the branches. Whoever abides in me and I in him, he it is that bears much fruit, for apart from me you can do nothing.
Say: Vines that are attached to the root get what they need to grow.

Ask the group to describe what happens if a branch is disconnected.

Acknowledge responses. Look for answers such as:
- It dies.
- It wilts.

Read this scripture out loud:

Revelation 3:20
Behold, I stand at the door and knock. If anyone hears my voice and opens the door, I will come in to him and eat with him, and he with me.

Ask the group to describe how it might feel to invite complete strangers into their homes to hang out for supper.
- Would you know what they like to eat?
- What would you talk about?

Acknowledge responses. Look for answers such as:
- You might cook something they didn't like.
- It would be awkward.

Say: When we are close to someone, it's easier to know what they like, how they think, and why they do certain things.

Point out it is usually the people we are close to that we trust.

Say: That's the kind of relationship God wants with us.

ACTIVITY

Answer questions as a group.

1   Day sixteen talked about our true identity. It said that we are uniquely made. You were challenged to identify one thing in your life that does not truly represent your lifestyle.

    What can you do to change that behavior?

2   Day seventeen talked about being a light for the Lord.

    Describe how others see the Lord in you.

    What is one thing you can do to "shine" for Jesus?

3   Day eighteen talked about what we can do when life gets hard. You were challenged to find one scripture that you could turn to when you are in a dark place.

    What is the scripture you wrote down?

4   Day twenty-one talked about a life that is fully surrendered to God. You were challenged to commit to surrendering one part of your life to God.

    What was your commitment?

Remind the group that this is an opportunity to help each other be accountable.

Ask them to share ways they can help each other.

WRAP UP

Say: Everyone has a choice to own their relationship with the Lord. We can sit on the fence, but eventually we need to decide which side we are on.

Read this scripture out loud:

Revelation 3:15
"I know your works: you are neither cold nor hot. Would that you were either cold or hot!"

Say: The Lord wants us to choose to be committed to him.

Remind the group there is so much to gain by pressing into their relationship with God.

Read this scripture out loud:

Jeremiah 33:3
Call to me and I will answer you, and will tell you great and hidden things that you have not known.

End in prayer

WEEK FIVE – OWNING YOUR FAITH

WEAPONS

Prayer
- God created and designed us for a purpose.
- God is writing our stories.

God's word:

Proverbs 3:5-6
Trust in the Lord with all your heart, and do not lean on your own understanding. In all your ways acknowledge him, and he will make straight your paths.

Praise <<Play a worship song of your choice.>>

ACTIVITY
2.5 minutes

Ask volunteers to share one item they have had for a long time (ex: a book, a picture, a blanket...) that is very special to them.

Acknowledge their answers.

Ask one or two volunteers to share why they keep that item.

The goal here is to get them to connect their love of the item with the reasons why they keep it.

CORE CONTENT

Point out that the things we feel are precious and important are the things we usually take care of and keep around us.

Say: When we believe something has value, we usually make sure it is kept safe. We wouldn't usually toss it in the garbage, or throw it someplace it might get lost.

Read this scripture out loud:

Psalm 119:105
Your word is a lamp to my feet and a light to my path.

Say: God's word helps keep us safe and on track. It is a lamp that lights up where we are right now, but it also lights up the road where we're going.

Read this scripture out loud:

Jeremiah 29:11
For I know the plans I have for you, declares the Lord, plans for welfare and not for evil, to give you a future and a hope.

Tell the group God's plan is that their lives might be complete and meaningful through him.

Say: There is no relationship more important than the one we have with the Lord.

Ask one or two volunteers what they think it means to "own" their faith?

There is no right or wrong answer. The goal here is to get them to identify how they personally own their relationship with the Lord.

ACTIVITY

Answer questions as a group.

1. Day twenty-two talked about the desires of our heart. You were challenged to name one or two "desires of your heart."
   - How did what you wrote surprise you?

   - What did you write down that you already knew about?

   - Share one thing you wrote with the group.

2. Day twenty-three talked about understanding our purpose.

   How do you live out your purpose in everyday life?

3. Day twenty-four talked about turning fear into faith. You were challenged to write down one fear that you would surrender to the Lord, then to rip, burn, or shred it.

   - Describe how it felt writing down your fear.

   - Describe the feeling of destroying it.

4. Day twenty-five talked about sharing your faith with others.

   - Who did you share your faith with this week?

   - If you didn't share with someone, name the person you'll reach out to next week.

5. Day twenty-six talked about participating in the gospel. What does it mean to be an example in our faith?

6. Day twenty-seven talked about having the confidence to share your faith.

   - How are we equipped to share our faith?

7. Day twenty-eight talked about what it means to live a gospel-centered life.
   - Describe what that means to you.

WRAP UP

Remind the group that God is the author of their stories. He will continue to write new chapters every day.

Encourage them to keep seeking out the truth in God's word about their stories.

End in prayer

WEEK SIX – MAKING IT STICK

Instructor note:

Making it Stick day is an opportunity for the group to reflect on and begin to put into action the concepts they have learned throughout this study.

This week is activity driven. The session begins with the "Weapons" section, goes into a short "Core Content" section, then is followed by the activities.

Instructions for several activities are included. Feel free to shift any activity to fit group dynamics, event location, or time allotment. In addition, you can eliminate any activity based on time.

WEAPONS

Prayer:
- God is never done with us on this side of heaven.
- God is writing your story.

God's word:

Romans 8:28
And we know that for those who love God all things work together for good, for those who are called according to his purpose.

Praise: <<Play a worship song of your choice.>>

CORE CONTENT

Say: Over the last few weeks we've had an opportunity to dig into our faith. There may have been struggles, and it may not have been perfect, but that is okay.

Point out when we repeatedly doing something over and over it becomes a habit.

Ask two or three volunteers to share one takeaway from the study.

Encourage everyone to share one thing they learned.

Say: When learning new ways to do things or accomplishing something important, it's easy to move past it and jump into the next thing. Celebrating what we've done is a good way to mark it as a milestone.

It's important to commemorate what we accomplish. It helps us remember where we've had victory.

Point out that remembering the battles we've won does two things:

- It helps us celebrate victories. Many small wins add up to big success!
- It helps us when we struggle. Somewhere down the road we may hit a long boring plateau, find ourselves in a dry desert, or struggle to climb the mountain in front of us. In that moment, revisiting the victories we've had can give us confidence to keep going.

Point out the Bible has many examples where we are encouraged to remember.

Read these scriptures out loud:

Psalm 77:11
I will remember the deeds of the LORD; yes, I will remember your wonders of old.

2 Thessalonians 2:15
So then, brothers, stand firm and hold to the traditions that you were taught by us, either by our spoken word or by our letter.

ACTIVITIES

Activity One
10 minutes

Preparation prior to class:
For this activity, individuals will need a notebook or journal for week six of class. Purchase one notebook/ journal for each participant.

As an alternative, you can ask each participant to bring a new journal or notebook to class.

1. Instruct individuals to write their names on their notebooks or journals.

2. Tell them to pass their journals to the individual sitting on their right.

   - Have the person on their right write a word of encouragement in the journal for the owner.
   - After one minute, have them close the book and pass it back to the owner.
   - Tell the owners not to peek at what was written.

3. Tell individuals to now pass their journals to the individual sitting on their left.
   - Have the person on their left write a word of encouragement to the journal owner.
   - After one minute, have them close the book and pass it back to the owner.

4. Give the class a moment to read what was written in their journals.

Ask individuals if the words that were written surprised them.

Have one or two volunteers share how the words written impacted them.

Say: It's important to have the right people around you that will encourage and lift you up.

Ask volunteers to share how having encouragement would change their journey going forward.

Allow one or two volunteers to share.

Ask individuals to share ways they can continue to encourage one another after the study group ends.

Allow one or two volunteers to share.

Encourage individuals to stay connected to each other outside the group.

Activity Two
10 minutes

Preparation prior to class:
Prepare a playlist of one or two worship songs to play during the activity. You may use songs from previous weeks.

1. **Instruct** individuals to work on their own.
2. **Ask** them to quiet their minds and reflect on what they've been learning over the past weeks.
3. **Have** them write down some of the key points they've learned on a page in their journal.
4. **Remind** them not to chat with their neighbor if they finish early. Suggest they sit quietly (perhaps with eyes closed) to allow others to finish the activity.

Ask several volunteers (have the entire group share if time allows) to share the takeaway that most surprised them, and why it surprised them.

There are no right or wrong answers here, so remind the group to be open and allow time for anyone willing to share their words.

Have several volunteers share how it felt to reflect on what they learned.

Encourage individuals to continue to:
- Keep their journals near when they are home.
- Write down more things they remember from the group.
- Refer to their journals on days they struggle.
- Continue to write down what God shows them.

Activity Three
10 minutes

Preparation prior to class:
- Write scriptures from the *Own It* devotional on notecards.
- Make sure you have enough for everyone in the group.

1. **Hand** the stack to one attendee, face down.

2. **Ask** the person with the cards to:
   - **Take** one card.
   - **Keep** the card they took face down.
   - **Do not** look at it.
   - **Pass** the remaining notecards to the person on their left or right.

3. Once everyone has a notecard, **Have** the group turn over their card and read the scripture.

Ask several volunteers (have the entire group share if time allows) to share their scripture and how it relates to their own journey with the Lord.

Read this scripture out loud:

2 Samuel 7:28
And now, O Lord God, you are God, and your words are true, and you have promised this good thing to your servant.

Remind them that God's word is always relevant to our lives.

Activity Four
10 minutes

Preparation prior to class:
- Ask your pastor, youth leader, or other leadership or mentor to write a short letter of encouragement to the group.

- If possible, gather more than one letter.

1. **Read** the encouragement to the group.
2. **Ask** them to share how hearing those words made them feel.
3. **Have** them come up with ways they could encourage others.
4. **Remind** them we all need others around us.
5. **Ask** them to commit to finding ways to encourage and support others going through their own faith journey.

WRAP UP

Point out they have all learned about themselves and their faith journey over the previous weeks.

Ask for volunteers to share:
- How they will continue to grow in faith going forward.
- What they can do to stay plugged into their faith.
- Who they will connect with if they struggle, or need help.

Say: We have a choice in how we live out our faith. We can either sit back and hope it all works out, or we can dig in and own our faith journey.

Remind the group the journey they started over the last few weeks doesn't have to end when the group ends.

Point out that they may struggle from time-to-time, but they will continue to gain ground if they don't give up.

Read this scripture out loud:

2 Corinthians 13:11
Finally, brothers, rejoice. Aim for restoration, comfort one another, agree with one another, live in peace; and the God of love and peace will be with you.

Encourage the group to stay in God's Word daily.

Remind them to stay connected to each other and to build strong circles with friends, and leaders who are willing to help them grow.

Say: As you go forward, give yourself grace, knowing that the Lord will continue to challenge and grow you along the way.

End in Prayer

CONCLUSION

Every important journey of change begins when we take one step in a new direction. Without taking that first step, we will usually stay in the same place.

The thing is, it also takes *guts* to change. Many times, it means changing our habits, our thinking, and sometimes, even our friends.

But...

It's ALWAYS worth it!!

Owning your own faith may be something completely new to you, or it may be something you have been working on for a long time. No matter where you are in the process, it's going to change you in amazing ways!

So...

What we want to remind you is this...

Take a step,

      then another one,

          and another one....

This is going to be the best journey you've ever taken!

ABOUT THE AUTHORS

Cade Thompson, is an energetic and soulful Contemporary Christian music artist, with a sound that appeals to believers and mainstream pop audiences alike.

God has continued to reveal Cade's heart, and the outpouring has resulted in a strong connection to his generation sonically and lyrically.

Cade's love for people and his desire to reach generations is evident in his music, and his love for the people inspired by his music.

Follow Cade at: cadethompsonmusic.com, and on all social media platforms.

Shelley Furtado-Linton is an author, speaker, and mentor who uses life experiences to help individuals recognize and take hold of their God-given purpose and identity. She has a passion for those who are broken and held captive by difficult past experiences.

The insights gained through her own restoration journey, along with her passion for helping others find freedom through faith is the foundation for her writing, speaking, and ministry.

Follow Shelley at: shelleyfurtadolinton.com, and on all social media platforms.